ROMEO AND JULIET

To my sisters, Penny and Tina

Library of Congress Cataloging-in-Publication Data

Early, Margaret, 1951–
Romeo and Juliet / retold and illustrated by Margaret Early.
p.   cm.
Summary: A prose retelling of Shakespeare's drama in which young lovers
attempt to defy fate.
ISBN 0-8109-3799-9 (clothbound)
[1. Shakespeare, William, 1564–1616—Adaptations.]
I. Shakespeare, William, 1564–1616. Romeo and Juliet. II. Title.
PZ7.E12645Ro   1998
[Fic]–dc21   97–35366

First published in Australia in 1998 by Thomas C. Lothian Pty. Ltd.

Published in 1998 by Harry N. Abrams, Incorporated, New York
All rights reserved. No part of the contents of this book may be reproduced
without the written permission of the publisher.
Printed and bound in Hong Kong

 Harry N. Abrams, Inc.
100 Fifth Avenue
New York, N.Y. 10011
www.abramsbooks.com

THE MOST EXCELLENT AND LAMENTABLE TRAGEDY OF
ROMEO AND JULIET

Retold and illustrated
by
Margaret Early

Harry N. Abrams, Inc., Publishers

NCE UPON A TIME, in the fair city of Verona, lived two noble families, the Montagues and the Capulets. These great households possessed everything that life could offer, but there was no peace between them, for each hated the other worse than death. An ancient quarrel had existed between them for so long that nobody could remember when it had started, or even what had caused it. So great was the hatred between the two families, and even between their servants and followers, that whenever they met in public places or passed one another on the streets there was trouble. Angry glances would lead to fierce words, and fierce words too often led to fighting and bloodshed.

Such a quarrel occurred one hot summer day when two idle servants of the Capulet family, looking for mischief, saw two Montague servants in the market place and set upon them. Benvolio, a sensible young Montague, tried to stop the brawling, but he was attacked by Tybalt, a fiery young Capulet. Then the heads of both families appeared on the scene. They drew their swords and were about to join in the battle when there was a blast of trumpets and the Prince of Verona, followed by his soldiers, rode furiously into the market square. The constant fighting and brawling between the two warring families had disturbed the quiet of Verona's streets for too long, and now the Prince had had enough.

'Rebellious subjects, enemies to peace!' he roared, ordering the men to throw their weapons to the ground and threatening to severely punish anyone who disobeyed.

Having restored order, the Prince rebuked the combatants for their lawless behaviour and uttered this stern warning, before ordering them to leave the market place: 'If ever you disturb our streets again, your lives shall pay the forfeit.'

AS THE CROWD BEGAN to disperse, the wise Benvolio saw his cousin Romeo enter the marketplace, looking sad and forlorn. When asked why he was so downcast, Romeo told Benvolio that he had fallen in love with a girl called Rosaline, but she had rejected him and would have nothing to do with him. Benvolio laughed and told Romeo to forget this Rosaline: were he only to open his eyes and look about him he would find many other women in Verona equally fair. But the lovesick Romeo would have none of this. His devotion to Rosaline was so great, he vowed, he would never look at anyone else.

While the two friends were speaking, a stranger approached them, looking bewildered. His master was holding a great supper party at his house that night, he explained, and had given him a list of distinguished guests to invite, but he could not read.

When Romeo offered to help the poor fellow by reading out the list for him, whose name should he find there but that of his incomparable Rosaline! At whose house was the banquet to be? Romeo enquired.

'My master is the great rich Lord Capulet,' the servant replied. 'And if you are not of the house of Montague, I pray, come and crush a cup of wine.'

Such an invitation was tempting, but to accept would be dangerous. No Montague would dare to enter the house of the enemy Capulet. Even so, Benvolio eagerly encouraged Romeo to do just that. They could go to the feast together, disguised by masks, as was the custom for uninvited guests in those days. 'Go thither,' he urged, hoping to cure Romeo of his pitiful yearning for the disdainful Rosaline. He knew from the list of guests that some of the most admired ladies in Verona would be present, and among them would be some whose beauty would surely catch Romeo's eye. He would soon see for himself that there were other women in Verona far more beautiful than Rosaline. 'Compare her face with some that I will show,' Benvolio assured his cousin, 'and I will make thee think thy swan a crow.'

COUNT PARIS, a distinguished relative of the Prince of Verona, wished to marry Juliet, the only daughter of Lord Capulet. When asked if he would consent to give his daughter's hand in marriage, Lord Capulet replied that Juliet was too young. Why not wait a little longer? 'Let two more summers wither in their pride ere we may think her ripe to be a bride,' he entreated.

As was common in those days, the suitor had not yet met the woman he wanted to marry, nor she him, and so Lord Capulet invited Paris to the banquet at his house that night. 'Woo her, gentle Paris, get her heart,' he advised. However, like Benvolio, he knew there would be many other beautiful young women present. Though he called them 'Earth-treading stars that make dark heaven light,' he felt none was Juliet's equal.

That same day Lady Capulet called Juliet to her chamber to ask her daughter her thoughts on marriage. Had the idea entered her mind?

Not for a moment, Juliet told her. 'It is an honour that I dream not of,' she answered. She was not yet fourteen years old.

'But, Juliet, here in Verona, ladies of esteem, younger than you, are already mothers,' Lady Capulet reminded her, adding that she herself was married at Juliet's age. And then she came to the point, announcing the real reason she had summoned her daughter: 'The valiant Paris seeks you for his love.'

Juliet's old nurse was delighted to overhear this. She had always said that Juliet was the prettiest baby she had ever nursed, and her greatest wish was to live to see her married.

Lady Capulet told Juliet she would meet the noble Count Paris at the feast that night. She should take this opportunity to study his face, look into his eyes, and decide if she might have him for a husband.

HAT NIGHT, wearing masks to disguise their identity, Romeo, Benvolio and their friend Mercutio went to the feast at the house of the Capulets. Lord Capulet made the three mysterious strangers welcome. He was light-hearted and merry, and told them that he, too, had worn a mask when he was young, and had whispered stories in a fair lady's ear.

While watching the dancing, Romeo was suddenly struck by the great beauty of a particularly handsome young woman — and it was not Rosaline! He thought her the most exquisite creature he had ever seen. He was so enthralled that he could not resist saying aloud, 'Oh, she doth teach the torches to burn bright! I never saw true beauty till this night.'

It happened that Juliet's cousin, the fiery Tybalt, the Capulet who had fought with Benvolio in the market place that day, was standing close by. He recognised Romeo's voice at once. Furious that a Montague should dare to enter the house of Capulet, he gave vent to his anger and called for his sword, but his uncle, Lord Capulet, ordered him to contain his temper. Romeo had done no wrong, he declared. This young Montague was renowned throughout Verona for his gentlemanly conduct and good character and, as a guest in the Capulet household, he was entitled to be left in peace. Nothing was to disturb this night of revelry and feasting.

When the headstrong Tybalt answered back, his uncle banished him from the room and he left in anger, swearing vengeance against Romeo.

Romeo knew nothing of this, so enchanted was he by the vision of Juliet. He moved towards her and touched her hand. The two looked into each other's eyes, exchanged tender words, then kisses, and, within an instant, not even knowing each other's name, they fell in love.

At that moment Juliet's nurse interrupted the enraptured pair to announce, 'Madam, your mother craves a word with you.'

As Juliet reluctantly parted from her new-found love to seek out Lady Capulet, Romeo asked the nurse, 'What is her mother?'

'Her mother is the lady of the house,' was the reply.

Romeo was thunderstruck. He, a Montague, had fallen in love with the daughter of a Capulet!

Juliet, too, was about to be thunderstruck. As Romeo and his friends left the room she asked her nurse if she knew who the handsome young man was. The nurse replied, 'His name is Romeo, and a Montague, the only son of your great enemy.'

ATER THAT NIGHT Romeo climbed over the wall of an orchard behind Juliet's house, longing to see her and be near her once more. Presently a light appeared at an upstairs window and Juliet stepped onto the balcony which stood before it. Romeo was entranced. He saw her look up into the starry sky, and when he heard her sigh 'Oh, Romeo, Romeo! Wherefore art thou, Romeo?' he could hardly contain his excitement. Juliet went on, addressing the night, saying that it was only Romeo's name, not Romeo himself, that was her enemy. What difference should a mere name make? 'A rose by any other name would smell as sweet,' she declared. If only Romeo could cast off the Montague name so hated by every Capulet! 'Deny thy father and refuse thy name,' she wished aloud. Were he not a Montague he could be hers.

Romeo could restrain himself no longer. 'I take thee at thy word,' he called from the darkness below. 'Henceforth I never will be Romeo.'

Juliet was startled and alarmed by these words. Her innermost thoughts had been overheard. But by whom? She became even more fearful when she realised that the voice from the garden below was none other than Romeo's! She knew that, as a Montague, he would be killed if her kinsmen were to discover him there. Then she was embarrassed, knowing that he had heard her declare her love for him.

But Romeo assured her there was nothing to fear: the darkness of night would protect him and, as for the confession of love, so freely given, how much time that saved them!

Even so, fearing for his safety, Juliet begged her Romeo to leave without delay. She assured him of the depth of her love: 'My bounty is as boundless as the sea, my love as deep; the more I give to thee the more I have, for both are infinite.'

Suddenly there was a noise from inside. It was the nurse, calling for Juliet.

Quickly Juliet whispered to Romeo that if he meant all he said and wished to marry her, he was to send her a message the next day, telling her the time and place the wedding ceremony would be performed, adding: 'And all my fortunes at thy foot I'll lay, and follow thee, my lord, throughout the world. Good-night, good-night, parting is such sweet sorrow, that I shall say good-night till it be morrow.'

Romeo climbed back over the garden wall, all thought of Rosaline swept from his mind forever, while Juliet, for her part, went to bed with never a thought for the wealthy young Count Paris.

THE NEW DAY had begun to dawn when the lovers parted. Romeo was too full of thoughts of Juliet to be able to sleep, so instead of going home to bed he went straight to a monastery nearby to beg his confessor, Friar Lawrence, to marry him to his newly found love that very day.

The good friar assumed that Romeo's sleepless night must have been caused by thoughts of love for Rosaline, and was surprised to hear that it was Lord Capulet's daughter he now wished most fervently to marry. After considering the matter, and being assured by Romeo of the depth of his love for Juliet, and of Juliet for him, the friar decided that a marriage of a Montague to a Capulet might be the very means of bringing to an end the bitter feuding between the two families at last. And so he consented to perform the wedding ceremony in his cell in the monastery later that day.

While Romeo had been with the holy friar, Benvolio and Mercutio learned that Tybalt, mad for revenge, had left a letter at the Montague house, challenging Romeo to a duel to the death. When Romeo arrived on the scene in a cheerful mood, his friends were about to tell him of Tybalt's letter, but just then Juliet's nurse came along, her skirts billowing and bosom heaving as she strode majestically down the street, the wind catching her cloak and veil. The three friends made much fun of her, twirling her around and teasing her.

Panting for breath, the nurse asked where she could find a person called Romeo. Romeo stepped forward, bowed and introduced himself, while Benvolio and Mercutio walked away laughing. They had forgotten to warn Romeo about Tybalt's murderous letter.

The nurse, having learnt of Juliet's love for Romeo, begged him to be honest and true in his dealings with Juliet and not take unfair advantage of a girl so young and innocent. Romeo set her mind at ease in the most surprising way: he told the nurse to take Juliet his message that she was to come to Friar Lawrence's cell that afternoon, as though to confession, and that there they would be secretly married that very day.

Although the nurse knew that Juliet's parents wanted her to marry Count Paris, Romeo's announcement filled her with joy, for there was nothing she liked better than a wedding — and the sooner the better! And so she scurried off to carry this exciting news to her young mistress.

JULIET, WAITING IMPATIENTLY for the nurse's return, could hardly contain herself for want of news of her Romeo. The nurse had promised to be back within half an hour, and yet three hours had passed and still there was no sign of her.

When the nurse finally appeared, looking sour-faced, Juliet was beside herself with excitement. 'Oh honey Nurse, what news? Hast thou met with him?' she called.

But the nurse would not tell Juliet what she wanted to know, saying she was weary and needed rest. She complained about her tired bones and lack of breath.

Juliet was exasperated. 'How art thou out of breath, when thou hast breath to say to me that thou art out of breath?'

But still the nurse would not reveal the message her mistress was waiting so eagerly to hear. Instead, she kept on with a list of complaints: her head ached, and then her back; she spoke of this and that, and other matters, anything but Romeo's message of the secret wedding plan.

Juliet could stand it no longer. 'Come, what says Romeo? What says he of our marriage? Sweet, sweet, sweet Nurse, tell me, what says my love?'

At last the nurse stopped teasing Juliet and took pity on her. She told her she was to meet with Romeo that afternoon in Friar Lawrence's cell, where they would be married at once.

And so that day the two lovers were united in marriage. Juliet became a Montague and Romeo kinsman to the Capulets.

After the ceremony Juliet returned home to wait for nightfall, when once more Romeo would secretly come to her on the balcony.

THAT SAME DAY Benvolio and Mercutio were walking through the streets of Verona when they were met by Tybalt and other hostile Capulets. Angry words were being exchanged when Romeo suddenly appeared.

'Here comes my man,' said Tybalt and insulted Romeo, hoping to provoke a fight. He challenged Romeo to draw his sword, but Romeo refused. He knew nothing about Tybalt's letter, and having, within the hour, been married to Tybalt's cousin Juliet, he felt that he himself was now partly a Capulet. Because of that, he had no wish to fight Tybalt. However, as his marriage to Juliet was still secret, he could not explain his reasons to his friends.

Mercutio, not knowing this and therefore unable to understand why Romeo did not react to Tybalt's insults, now took it upon himself to defend the honour of the house of Montague. He attacked Tybalt furiously with his sword.

Romeo, aghast, tried to stop the fight, and pleaded with both men to put up their swords. He grabbed Mercutio's arm, trying to hold him back, but Tybalt seized the moment and thrust his sword into Mercutio's breast.

Mercutio died in Romeo's arms, cursing the houses of Montague and Capulet alike.

Romeo, now enraged, and without thinking of the consequences, drew his sword and killed Tybalt with one blow.

Alarmed by this terrifying turn of events, and mindful of the penalty of death that the Prince of Verona had decreed on anyone disturbing the public peace, Benvolio now urged Romeo to flee for his life.

FTER THE FIGHT, Romeo hastened to the nearby monastery, where he took sanctuary in Friar Lawrence's cell.

In due course he learned there that the Prince had been merciful. Rather than sentencing Romeo to death for breaking his decree, the Prince had ordered that he be banished from the fair city of Verona, never to set foot inside its walls again.

Romeo was distraught. This was a sentence worse than death. For him there was no world outside Verona, and no life without Juliet. Heaven was where Juliet lived; all else was purgatory and torture.

There was a knocking at the door, and Juliet's nurse entered. She had come to the monastery in haste to bring news to Romeo that his young bride was also in great distress, crying over his cruel banishment and wailing over the death of her dear cousin Tybalt, her sorrow made all the greater by knowing that it was her husband who had killed him.

Romeo's remorse now knew no bounds, but the good friar calmed him. He advised him to visit Juliet in secret, to take his farewell from her before leaving Verona without further delay. He should stay in exile in Mantua until the time was right for the friar to make their marriage public. He believed that such an announcement would unite the two families and bring their age-old conflict to an end. He also believed that, on hearing such news, the Prince of Verona would grant Romeo a pardon and allow him to return to the city. The friar promised to send letters to Romeo from time to time to let him know what was happening in Verona.

'Go, get thee to thy love as was decreed,' the friar urged at last. 'Ascend her chamber — hence and comfort her.'

ND SO ROMEO spent his wedding night with his beloved Juliet, having secretly climbed up to her room from the orchard below.

The whole night long the two lovers found sublime happiness and rapture in each other's arms. But all too soon it seemed the dawn was about to break and Romeo must leave, for it would be certain death were he to be found within Verona's walls. When Juliet heard the song of the lark outside her window she knew that it was almost morning but, not wanting Romeo to leave her, she pretended it was the voice of the nightingale and not the lark. 'Nightly she sings on yon pomegranate tree. Believe me, love, it was the nightingale.'

But Romeo knew the sad truth. 'It was the lark, the herald of the morn, no nightingale. I must be gone and live, or stay and die.'

So saying, he took a final kiss, climbed down from the balcony, bade Juliet farewell, and was gone, leaving her tearful and forlorn.

THIS WAS BUT THE BEGINNING of the tragedy for this pair of star-crossed lovers. In the following days the Capulet household echoed with Juliet's sobs and tears.

Everyone thought her great distress was for her dead cousin Tybalt, and only her nurse knew the real reason for it.

To put a stop to his daughter's tiresome wailing, Lord Capulet announced one Monday that he had arranged for her to marry Count Paris in three days' time.

Juliet was alarmed at this turn of events. How could her father know that she was already married — and, of all the people in the world, to a Montague! She tried to reason with him — she was too young; she was still grieving for her dear Tybalt; it would not be fitting to have a wedding so soon after her cousin's death — but her father would not listen.

When he stormed away angrily, Juliet pleaded with Lady Capulet: 'Oh, sweet my mother, cast me not away! Delay this marriage for a month, a week . . .'

But Lady Capulet rejected her daughter's desperate cry for help. 'Talk not to me,' she said, 'for I'll not speak a word. Do as thou wilt, for I have done with thee.' And she, too, departed in anger.

Juliet now turned to her nurse for comforting words, but there were none.

IN DESPERATION, Juliet hurried to the monastery to seek help from the friendly Friar Lawrence, who had always given her good counsel in times of trouble. To him she now revealed the depth of her misery and despair.

The good friar was so moved by Juliet's love for Romeo that he devised a plan to save her from marriage to Count Paris. He gave her a small flask containing a curious liquid which, when she swallowed it on the eve of the proposed wedding to Paris, would put her into such a deep sleep that, the next morning, having neither pulse, warmth nor breath, she would seem to all the world to be dead. Then, as was the custom, her body would be taken to the ancient Capulet vault, clothed in the finest robes, to await burial. And there, forty-two hours after taking the mysterious liquid, she would suddenly awaken, miraculously, as from a pleasant sleep, to find her Romeo waiting for her.

'He and I will watch thy waking, and that very night shall Romeo bear thee hence to Mantua,' the friar assured her. 'Now get you gone, be strong in this resolve. I'll send a messenger with speed to Mantua with my letter to thy Romeo.'

When she returned to her house, Juliet told her father that she was now willing to marry Paris. Lord Capulet was delighted at his daughter's change of heart. He ordered the household to begin preparing for a grand wedding, to take place the next day.

That night, standing alone in her room, the flask of liquid in her hand, Juliet began to have doubts about the friar's plan. Had he really given her a deadly poison in order to kill her, thus saving himself from dishonour for having secretly married a Capulet to a Montague? But no, that could not be; the friar was known to be a good and holy man. Then she feared she might wake before Romeo arrived and be stifled in the airless vault, surrounded by the bones of all her ancestors, with the body of her dead cousin Tybalt lying beside her. And then she remembered all the fearful stories she had heard of ghosts that had haunted the family tomb for centuries.

Finally she took courage and swallowed the friar's potion, saying, 'Romeo, I come! This do I drink to thee.' And with that she threw herself onto her bed and at once fell into a deep sleep.

LOUD WERE THE SHRIEKS and wails from Juliet's nurse when she discovered the lifeless body of her mistress the next morning, lying cold, white and still on her bed, like a corpse.

Paris was heartbroken to learn of the apparent death of his intended bride, and great was the grief of Lord and Lady Capulet, for Juliet was their only child. They had loved her, and now death had taken her from them, just as she was about to be married.

Everything that had been prepared for a great wedding was now to be used for a funeral. Instead of the priest marrying Juliet that day, he would be obliged to bury her.

Friar Lawrence did not grieve. He knew that his letter was speeding on its way to Mantua, telling Romeo about the secret potion, the reason for it, and the need for him to come to Verona at once to be at Juliet's side at the moment of awakening. But bad news travels faster than good, and the messenger who arrived in Mantua that morning was not the friar's man — he had been prevented from leaving Verona — but Romeo's servant, who informed him that Juliet was dead.

Romeo, devastated and pale, whispered, 'Well, Juliet, I will lie with thee tonight.' And so, from an apothecary known to him, he purchased some poison strong enough to kill twenty men, and set off on horseback for Verona and Juliet's tomb.

AS SOON AS HE ENTERED the Capulet tomb, Romeo's eyes confirmed what his servant had told him. Juliet's lifeless body, cold and white, lay on a bed of stone before him. He had no reason to suspect that she might merely be asleep. He knelt beside her. 'Oh, my love! My wife! Death hath had no power yet upon thy beauty. I will stay with thee and never from this palace of dim night depart again. Eyes, look your last! Arms, take your last embrace!' he said. Then, lifting the poison to his mouth, he bade Juliet, and the world, farewell. 'Here's to my love! Thus with a kiss I die.'

Not long afterwards Juliet began to wake from her heavy sleep, calling Romeo's name. She was horrified to see her husband lying dead before her! When she saw the cup from which he had drunk she understood at once what had happened, what a terrible mistake had been made. She took the vessel from his hand, hoping to find some dregs of poison still in it, for without Romeo she no longer wished to live. But there was none. 'Drunk all,' she pined, 'and left no friendly drop to help me after.' Then she kissed Romeo's lips, thinking there might still be poison left on them, but again there was none. So she took Romeo's dagger and drove it into her heart. 'There rest, and let me die,' she gasped, as she fell on Romeo's body.

Word of the tragedy soon spread through all Verona, and a great crowd gathered at the Capulet monument. There, in the presence of all the Montagues and Capulets and the Prince of Verona, Friar Lawrence explained the full story of the tragedy of the star-crossed lovers, and the willing part he had played in it. The parents were grief-stricken by the tragic deaths of their only children, and ashamed of the old hatreds and rivalries that had led to such a disastrous end. In remorse they shook hands and embraced, and agreed to bury their ancient quarrel in their children's graves. Now linked together through the marriage of their dead children, the two families vowed to live in peace, harmony and friendship for ever more.

NOTES

WILLIAM SHAKESPEARE wrote *Romeo and Juliet* just over four hundred years ago, in 1595. His play was based on *The Tragicall Historye of Romeus and Juliet*, a poem written by Arthur Brooke thirty-three years earlier. The story had previously been treated in Italian by Masuccio of Salerno (1476), Luigi da Porto (1530) and Bandello (1554) and translated into French by Boaistuau (1559), from whom Brooke made his version. The full title, *The Most Excellent and Lamentable Tragedy of Romeo and Juliet*, dates from the 1599 second quarto edition of Shakespeare's play.

The setting for the action of *Romeo and Juliet* is the city of Verona in the year 1302. During the Middle Ages, Italian cities were often troubled by violent disagreements among their citizens. There were two rival political factions, the Guelphs, who supported supreme rule by the pope, and the Ghibellines, who favoured rule by the Holy Roman Emperor (who was German). Romeo belonged to the Montecchi (Montague) family, who were Guelphs, while Juliet, a Capulet, was a Ghibelline and therefore, by tradition, his enemy.

The illustrations in this edition have their inspiration in many sources. The backgrounds, courtyards, pavements and architectural details are derived from direct observation, sketches and studies made in the streets and buildings of Verona itself, as well as other Medieval cities. Various small details have their origins in frescoes by Mantegna (Palazzo Ducale, Mantua), Giotto (Florence), and Lorenzetti (Palazzo Publico, Siena), and paintings by Renaissance artists such as Michelangelo, Piero della Francesca, Pisanello, Veneziano, and Botticelli.

The illustrations were done in oils on synthetic canvas using, besides gold and white, only six colours: two reds, two yellows and two blues. The book is printed in five colours, the fifth being gold, for which I have made separate plates by hand.

Margaret Early